3 SECTIONS

Books by Vijay Seshadri

Wild Kingdom
The Long Meadow
The Disappearances
3 Sections

3 SECTIONS

Poems

Vijay Seshadri

Graywolf Press

This publication is made possible, in part, by the voters of Minnesota through
a Minnesota State Arts Board Operating Support grant, thanks to a legislative
appropriation from the arts and cultural heritage fund, and through a grant from
the Wells Fargo Foundation Minnesota. Significant support has also been provided by
Target, the McKnight Foundation, Amazon.com, and other generous contributions
from foundations, corporations, and individuals. To these organizations and individuals
we offer our heartfelt thanks.

Published by Graywolf Press
250 Third Avenue North, Suite 600
Minneapolis, Minnesota 55401

www.graywolfpress.org

Published in the United States of America

ISBN 978-1-55597-662-0 (cloth)
ISBN 978-1-55597-716-0 (paper)

4 6 8 9 7 5 3

Library of Congress Control Number: 2014949446

Cover design: Jeenee Lee Design

for Nicholas

Contents

Imaginary Number   3

Rereading   4

Trailing Clouds of Glory   5

The Dream I Didn't Have   7

Memoir   8

This Morning   9

Surveillance Report   10

Hell   12

Purgatory, the Film   13

Purgatory, the Sequel   14

Heaven   15

Three Urdu Poems   16

Mixed-Media Botanical Drawing   19

New Media   20

Script Meeting   21

Secret Police   23

Guide for the Perplexed   25

Family Happiness   26

Elegy   27

As If   28

Nursing Home   29

Life of Savage   32

Thought Problem   33

Yet Another Scandal   34

Bright Copper Kettles   35

A School Day in October   36

Visiting Paris   37

Three Persons   38

The Descent of Man   39

Knowing   40

The People I Know   41

Pacific Fishes of Canada   43

Personal Essay   56

Light Verse   72

3 SECTIONS

Imaginary Number

The mountain that remains when the universe is destroyed
is not big and is not small.
Big and small are

comparative categories, and to what
could the mountain that remains when the universe is destroyed
be compared?

Consciousness observes and is appeased.
The soul scrambles across the screes.
The soul,

like the square root of minus 1,
is an impossibility that has its uses.

Rereading

Remember that family who lived in a boat
run aground and capsized
by the creamy dunes where the plovers nest?
Sea, sun, storm, and firmament
kept their minds occupied.
David Copperfield came and went,
and their sympathy for him was such
that they pitied him almost as much
as he pitied himself. But their story
is not like the easy one
where you return to me and
lift my scarred eyes to the sun
and stroke my withered hand
and marry me, distorted as I am.
He was destined to dismantle their lives,
David Copperfield, with his
treacherous friend and insipid wives,
his well-thought-out position
on the Corn Laws and the constitution.
They were stillness and
he was all motion.
They lived in a boat upside down on the strand,
but he was of the kind who couldn't understand
that land was not just land
or ocean ocean.

Trailing Clouds of Glory

Even though I'm an immigrant,
the angel with the flaming sword seems fine with me.
He unhooks the velvet rope. He ushers me into the club.
Some activity in the mosh pit, a banquet here, a panhandler there,
a gray curtain drawn down over the infinitely curving lunette,
Jupiter in its crescent phase, huge,
a vista of a waterfall, with a rainbow in the spray,
a few desultory orgies, a billboard
of the snub-nosed electric car of the future—
the inside is exactly the same as the outside,
down to the m.c. in the yellow spats.
So why the angel with the flaming sword
bringing in the sheep and waving away the goats,
and the men with the binoculars,
elbows resting on the roll bars of jeeps,
peering into the desert? There is a border,
but it is not fixed, it wavers, it shimmies, it rises
and plunges into the unimaginable seventh dimension
before erupting in a field of Dakota corn. On the F train
to Manhattan yesterday, I sat across
from a family threesome Guatemalan by the look of them—
delicate and archaic and Mayan—
and obviously undocumented to the bone.
They didn't seem anxious. The mother was
laughing and squabbling with the daughter
over a knockoff smart phone on which they were playing a
video game together. The boy, maybe three,
disdained their ruckus. I recognized the scowl on his face,
the retrospective, maskless rage of inception.
He looked just like my son when my son came out of his mother

after thirty hours of labor—the head squashed,
the lips swollen, the skin empurpled and hideous
with blood and afterbirth. Out of the inflamed tunnel
and into the cold room of harsh sounds.
He looked right at me with his bleared eyes.
He had a voice like Richard Burton's.
He had an impressive command of the major English texts.
I will do such things, what they are yet I know not,
but they shall be the terrors of the earth, he said.
The child, he said, *is father of the man.*

The Dream I Didn't Have

I woke up on the stainless-steel autopsy table.
My chest was weighted down.
Bodily fluids stained my paper hospital gown.
My life readings were stable,

though. They were, in fact, decisive—
one round number and one simple line.
A cop gave the coroner a form to sign,
but he lingered undecided over me,

murmuring to himself,
"That must have been a dream, or was it a vision?"
I felt along my length his long riverine incision.
Outside it was Chicago—

city of world-class museums,
handsome architecture, marvelous elevated trains—
rising from the plains
by the impossibly flat lake.

Memoir

Orwell says somewhere that no one ever writes the real story of their life.
The real story of a life is the story of its humiliations.
If I wrote that story now—
radioactive to the end of time—
people, I swear, your eyes would fall out, you couldn't peel
the gloves fast enough
from your hands scorched by the firestorms of that shame.
Your poor hands. Your poor eyes
to see me weeping in my room
or boring the tall blonde to death.
Once I accused the innocent.
Once I bowed and prayed to the guilty.
I still wince at what I once said to the devastated widow.
And one October afternoon, under a locust tree
whose blackened pods were falling and making
illuminating patterns on the pathway,
I was seized by joy,
and someone saw me there,
and that was the worst of all,
lacerating and unforgettable.

This Morning

First I had three
apocalyptic visions, each more terrible than the last.
The graves open, and the sea rises to kill us all.
Then the doorbell rang, and I went downstairs and signed for two packages—
one just an envelope, but the other long and bulky, difficult to manage—
both for my neighbor Gus. "You're never not at home,"
the FedEx guy said appreciatively.
It's true. I don't shave, or even wash. I keep the air-conditioners roaring.

Though it's summer,
one of the beautiful red-and-conifer-green Bayside Fuel Oil trucks
that bed down in the depot by the canal
was refreshing the subsurface tanks with black draughts
wrung from the rock, blood of the rock
sucked up from the crevices.
The driver looked unconcerned. Leaning slightly on each other,
Frank and Louise stepped over his hose and walked by slowly,
on the way to their cardiologist.

Surveillance Report

The omni-directional mike and the video camera, both tiny,
hidden in the bonsai cypress
are picking up my sunrise self-help talk show,
in the makeshift kitchen studio, in a bathrobe and bunny slippers.
First the opening monologue,
then the body banters with the mind, then queue up the callers.
Caller X is unhappy with the latest dream interpretation.
Caller X is cut off with a flick of the wrist.
Caller Y wants to share that my fearless candor has given her permission
to become utterly transparent herself.
Thank you, Caller Y. Your inner light can be seen from here.
Night-visiting revenants, clerks of the underworld,
gnawing the half-buried roots of being,
spirits of the burning trees, kiss me goodbye.
The tape shows me checking my chronometer and exiting for work.
Observers posted along my morning commute observe the usual detours,
the purchase of potables and comestibles.
Flash forward the digital feed.
At ten hundred hours, the current workplace asset texts,
"Subject agitated. Begging colleagues,
'Please have the courtesy not to be conscious of me.'"
Of the three or four scenarios employed
to predict my next location, during the interminable lunch hour,
when the terrible questions of where to go and what to eat
among choices once enticing but now exposed in all their bitter banality
assault even the most cheerful of our targets,
today, which is a Tuesday, is burning-house-scenario day.
Cloud after cloud of smoke and flames
sweep through and over the turrets,
the widow's walk, the pergolas, the port-cochere.

Fire boiling through the leaded windowpanes immolates the gillyflowers.
Though I haven't been located, for reasons I don't understand,
in the crowd shots pirated from the Eyewitness News feed,
what the crowd feels I would feel if I were there to feel it.
But I'm not there to feel it,
I'm not there at all, there at the next disaster,
the last disaster but one but one but one . . .
The dormant listening posts activate.
Windowless vans crammed with information technology
park on the corners of all the streets.
Oh, the wailing in the control room, the recriminations,
the pointing of fingers, the blame game, the pleas
of the pragmatic to move forward, not backward, and solve this problem,
find me and put me back on the grid.
Where will I be scanned for first? Maybe I'm in the trashed, padlocked
public restroom in the park. The pipes are hissing.
The concrete floor is littered with syringes and treacherous
with pools of chill and fetid standing water.
The mirrors are shattered, and the sinks and urinals are shattered.
This is the restroom nobody ever visits
in the park abandoned by humankind,
the dead zone where the transducer and the infrared lens quail,
where all the signals ricochet.
Or, alternatively, I could be on a beach somewhere.

Hell

You'd have to be as crazy as Dante to get those down,
the infernal hatreds.
Shoot them. Shoot them where they live
and then skip town.

Or stay and re-engineer
the decrepit social contraption
to distill the 200-proof
elixir of fear

and torture the . . . the what
from the what? And didn't I promise,
under threat of self-intubation,
not to envision this

corridor, coal-tar black,
that narrows down and in
to a shattering claustrophobia attack
before opening out

to the lake of frozen shit
where the gruesome figure is discerned?
Turn around, go home.
Just to look at it is to become it.

Purgatory, the Film

He was chronically out of work, why we don't know.
She was the second born of a set
of estranged identical twins. They met,
hooked up, and moved in with her mother,
who managed a motel on Skyline Drive.
But always it was the other,
the firstborn, the bad twin, the runaway,
he imagined in the shadow
of the "Vacancy" sign
or watching through the window
below the dripping eaves
while they made love or slept.
The body is relaxed and at rest,
the mind is relaxed in its nest,
so the self that is and is not
itself rises and leaves
to peek over the horizon, where it sees
all its psychokinetic possibilities
resolving into shapely fictions.
She was brave, nurturing, kind.
She was evil. She was out of her mind.
She was a junkie trading sex for a fix,
a chief executive, an aviatrix.
She was an angel
to the blinded and the lamed,
the less-than-upright, the infra dig.
And she was even a failure.
She went to LA to make it big
and crept back home injured and ashamed.

Purgatory, the Sequel

They put him in jail, why we don't know.
They stamped him "Postponed."
But he didn't mind.
The screws were almost kind.
He had leisure to get his muscles toned,

mental space to regret his crimes,
and when he wasn't fabricating license plates
he was free
to remember the beauty
that not once but a thousand times

escaped him forever, and escapes me, too:
ghosts of a mist drifting
across the face of the stars,
Jupiter triangulating
with the crescent moon and Mars,
prismatic fracturings in a drop of dew . . .

Heaven

There's drought on the mountain.
Wildfires scour the hills.
So the mammal crawls down the desiccated rills
searching for the fountain,

which it finds, believe it or not,
or sort of finds. A thin silver sliver
rises from an underground river
and makes a few of the hot

rocks steam and the pebbles hiss.
Soon the mammal will drink,
but it has first
to stop and think
its reflexive, impeccable thought:
that thinking comes down to this—
mystery, longing, thirst.

Three Urdu Poems

1. Mirza Ghalib

No, I wasn't meant to love and be loved.
If I'd lived longer, I would have waited longer.

Knowing you are faithless keeps me alive and hungry.
Knowing you faithful would kill me with joy.

Delicate are you, and your vows are delicate, too,
so easily do they break.

You are a laconic marksman. You leave me
not dead but perpetually dying.

I want my friends to heal me, succor me.
Instead, I get analysis.

Conflagrations that would make stones drip blood
are campfires compared to my anguish.

Two-headed, inescapable anguish!—
Love's anguish or the anguish of time.

Another dark, severing, incommunicable night.
Death would be fine, if I only died once.

I would have liked a solitary death,
not this lavish funeral, this grave anyone can visit.

You are mystical, Ghalib, and, also, you speak beautifully.
Are you a saint, or just drunk as usual?

2. Momin Khan Momin

My cause doesn't affect her, and, even worse,
the pain I feel doesn't cause pleasure.

I'm not that far gone. I still prefer
hearing she betrays me to her betraying me.

The very cosmos is thwarted because
in none of the ways you could be mine are you mine.

I don't know why she still keeps my heart,
as useless to her as an unpaired sandal.

Fate abhors me and I abhor fate,
and prayer can't reconcile us.

It's as if you're with me when I'm alone.
It's as if I'm alone when you're with me.

Momin, you're really a piece of work.
Is she God that you should kiss the hem of her garment?

3. Mirza Ghalib

How few, how paltry few, of all the beautiful apparitions pulverized to earth
were resurrected as a tulip or a rose.

How many of my glittering memories of the feast of love
were warehoused in oblivion.

The stars, bashful behind the veil of day,
what possesses them to become scandalous by night?

The father pining for the child sold to Pharaoh,
his eyes have become the windows of the walls that immure him.

I'm sorry, but I'm not like that woman who loved those who loved
whom she loved. The opposite, in fact.

The night is his who spends it coiled with you.

O citizens, if Ghalib keeps weeping like this,
his tears will sweep your cities away.

Mixed-Media Botanical Drawing

Contorted blossoms, slack,
lascivious orchids,
the tulip's petal so saturated with purple
that it looks black,

the ah-weary-of-time sunflower
crazed by living like a weed
next to the railroad spur,
periwinkles, peonies—

why them? Why them instead of
nothing at all? Well, who cares, really?
Only the feeling they excite counts.
It might be love,

it might not. The grafted rose bleeds
clear liquid at the sutured places.
It's a face, just one face,
in the middle of all the faces.

New Media

Why I wanted to escape experience is nobody's business but my own,
but I always believed I could if I could

put experience into words.
Now I know better.
Now I know words are experience.

"But ah thought kills me that I am not thought"
"2 People Searched for You"
"In the beginning was the . . ."
"re: Miss Exotic World"
"I Want Us To Executed Transaction"

It's not the thing,
there is no thing,
there's no thing in itself,
there's nothing but what's said about the thing,
there are no things but words

about the things
said over and over,
perching, grooming their wings,
on the subject lines.

Script Meeting

So, there's this guy—what is he, forty, fifty?
He has a condition, a history. Exurban, depressed, but alert,
his senses are sharp.
He hears the little hiccups embedded in the pattern of sound.
Sleep-walking in the woods,
premonitions of cataclysms,
flashbacks to black ops—
all of which you do a nice job of establishing under the opening credits—
dimple, we might say, the emptiness of his days.
And, then, next, cue the family memories:
the accident on I-5,
the eighteen-wheeler, rain, fog, a doe;
the lake, the stalled outboard motor, the rogue wave;
the explosion in the warehouse,
which is very good,
something needs to be blown up right about here.
But we have to know what actually happened sooner
rather than later. Remember,
our reputation as a studio is built not on suspense
but on horror.
We like the genetically engineered second wife and son.
The zombie in the basement, not so much.
Only a little bit less tedious than
his guilt-soaked diary entries in a fine copperplate hand
are the drooling flashes of nobility interspersing his psychotic episodes.
You have his eyeballs
twitching out of their sockets right here,
and how many times have we seen that before, how many times
have we left the multiplex disappointed,
convinced our needs will never be satisfied by

the world's mimetic gestures?
Don't leave us feeling like that. Stick with your guy.
He's his own zombie.
He haunts his own nights.
Not in this life will he tear himself from the bank of the burning river,
hotfooting it on the radiating marl
as his arrow of longing seeks the other shore.
Not in this life, or the next. Show us
what that means to him and what he means to it.
As our master said so long ago
in the London drawing room brilliant with candelabras,
"Here let us linger as the coal-fired Victorian ambience
curses outside.
Never forget that both in art and that which art comprehends
the whom you create is the key,
it is to the whom you create that the what,
after all so trivial, so adventitious, upon examination,
will, or, as likely, will not, happen.
The rest we can manage digitally."

Secret Police

The towelette flutters punctually in the window.
The neighbor who never talks silently combusts on his patio
in choreographed figure eights.
The phone clicks: Click, click—Click, click.
"What's that sound? Is it you or is it I?"
It's not you, and it's not me. Just the fact of the phone,
a turquoise Western Electric "Princess" model featuring
the "revolutionary" illuminated rotary dial,
so misplaced, frightening, and antediluvian
on this our tablescape of austere futurity, proves
that it is the secret police.
Who else could make the timelines intersect
and riddle them with emphasis and coincidence?
Is there a message? Are they toying with us?
A whole season is passing during which
the evidentiary, not to say allegorical,
nature of our experience, along with the vast conspiracies
therein implied, is making itself apparent
in a series of incidents the naïve would call accidental
but in which we can detect the presence
of the secret police. He says that's not his name,
when you know it's his name.
She in whose frank gaze
you were wont to drown now averts her eyes.
Don't even get me started on our co-workers,
whose sinuosities are instinct with a prevaricating design;
or on the subway in the sand;
or on the reason why I forget what I should remember
and remember what I should forget;
or on the flamingos that dart like sparrows

and soar and dive and congregate
in this our city, birdless until now since time began.
A shimmering, as in a mirage. A darkening, as in an aftermath.
A white light, then a red light, then a black light,
and then the meaning I mean, the meaning, and its meaning,
which I am just about to grasp.
Governments are falling as we speak.

Guide for the Perplexed

The bedroom slippers' silk linings.
The dressing gown of brocade, stitched with the zodiac.
The pajamas underneath also made out of silk,
for which how many individuals of the species *B. mori,*
having munched the succulent, pale-green mulberry leaves
and insinuated a sack wherein to magnify themselves,
were steamed to death from the inside out?
The delicate fibres are intact.
He feels their ripeness on his skin.
He listens deeply into the night, which listens back.
The birch log pops in the fireplace.
The fetishes brood on the mantelpiece.
The ice melts in the gin.
And yellower and deeper than dandelion yellow,
yellower and stronger than Moroccan yellow,
the color, almost, of a yellow marigold, is
the yellow silk kimono she wears to greet the floating world.
Moths on the wing clutter the starlight.
Ghosts of dead moths are on the windowpane and
knee deep in the ballroom,
in social clubs and places of worship.
They are proof, if anyone still needs proof, that
awesome are the powers of humankind,
who have taken this selfsame moth
and endowed it with a gene from the jellyfish
so as to produce fluorescent silk!
And all in the interests of beauty!
(I shall spare you, by the way,
my exhaustive researches into the history
of the Silk Road.)

Family Happiness

On our first date, I told my wife
I was a lesbian trapped in the body of a man.
Everybody says that now, of course,
on TV and radio, alternative media outlets,
tattoos and bumper stickers, but this was long ago, when
none but the brave (who deserve the fair)
would come up with something like that.
She smiled the pleased and goofy smile that flowers in her big eyes,
and I thought I had her.
Looking back now, though,
I can see her appraisal of me rounding to completeness.
I can hear her cognition firing.
She knew it. She knew even then
the truth it has cost me the aeons to acquire,
climbing and climbing the broken stairs:
I'm a man trapped in the body of a man.
I clutch the smooth walls and see through his eyes
the oil fires and containment units,
the huge clawed gantries strung out on the twilit polar horizon.
Through his alloyed ears, I hear
the objects of his scorn, his compassion, his hatred, his love
crying out and crying out.
Half my arms are his arms.
Half my face is welded to his face.
The other half mouths his clumsy ironies.
"Life is war," he says.
"Tragic," he says. "Tragic."
The simulacra are marching everywhere,
and deep in the caves the chimeras are breathing.

Elegy

I've been asked to instruct you about the town you've gone to,
where I've never been.
The cathedral is worth looking at,
but the streets are narrow, uneven, and a little grim.
The river is sluggish in the summer and muddy in the spring.
The cottage industries are obsolete.
The population numbers one.

The population numbers one fugitive
who slips into the shadows and haunts the belfries.
His half-eaten meals are cold on the empty café tables.
His page of unsolved equations is blowing down the cobblestones.
His death was so unjust that he can't forgive himself.
He waits for his life to catch up to him.

He is you and you and you.
You will look to him for your expiation,
face him in the revolving door, sit with him in the plaza
and soothe his fears and sympathize with his story
and accustom him to the overwhelming sun
until his death becomes your death.
You will restore his confiscated minutes to him one by one.

As If

Mother is excavating tissue from deep
in her cerebral mines.
Father is crying in his sleep.
The terrible family secret
that won't be exposed in these lines—
because there is no terrible family secret—
has Sister and Brother
raving at each other.
Finally to dissect
the well-meant lies
and realize
there's nothing underneath,
nothing to reveal,
and nothing is real
but these facts, bright and emphatic—
Mother in her cave and Father sleeping;
Mother in oblivion and Father weeping;
Sister and Brother forever searching the attic
for the terrible family secret
that is not, and never was,
and is the cause, is the cause . . .

Nursing Home

1.

She had dreams fifty years ago
she remembers on this day.
She dreamed about Bombay.
It looked like Rio.
She dreamed about Rio,

which looked like itself, though
Rio was a city she'd never seen—
not on TV, not in a magazine.
Brain scans done on her show

her perisylvian pathways and declivities
choked by cities,
microscopic mercurial cities
made from her memories,

good and bad,
from the things she saw but didn't see,
from the remembered pressure
of every lover she ever had.

2.

Unexpected useful combinations between cognitive psychology and neuroscience
have fostered new observational protocols not only for elderly patients in the Lewy
body pathologic subgroup but those discovered across a wide spectrum of demen-
tias and dementia-induced phenomena, including but not limited to Normal Pressure

Hydrocephalus (NPH), classical Alzheimer's disease (AD), and the deformations in mental recognition and function *(Dear, eat the soup with the spoon, not the fork)*, the coruscating visions *(Who is that laid out in my bed?)*, the spontaneous motor features of Parkinsonism. Synaptic patterns embodied in sparks, showers, electrical cascades, waterfalls, and shooting stars are increasingly revealing an etiology proximately to be fully established and suggestive links between processes strictly biochemical and ideational and linguistic explosions for which documentation has been massive while analysis has, so far, been scant. While an adequate conceptual apparatus still remains out of reach, progress across a broad frontier of research has been sufficiently dramatic to suggest possible developments that will lead both to therapeutic remedies for distressed elderly patients and to a synthesis among various disciplines that have heretofore seemed not just incompatible but in direct conflict with one another. Certain coherencies have been unearthed that have truly startled our consensus . . .

3.

—She doesn't know any better than to act the fool.

—Is she dead? No, she's not dead.

—Is she dead?

—No, I'm not dead, and I don't want anybody to think I'm dead.

—Do you think it's funny?

—Wonder why she acts like that?

—Is she dead? No, she's not dead, and I'm not dead, neither.

—Is she really dead? No, she's not dead, but she's acting the fool.

—Are you really dead? No, I'm not really dead. I'm just acting the fool.

—I'll show you how I can act the fool.

—No, I don't think I look nice. I think I look purty.

—No, I'm not dead. I just act like I'm dead.

—What makes you want to act like she's dead?

—Do you think she's dead?

—Do you think she's dead, or is she just acting the fool?

Life of Savage

I've been excited about him as an individual.
I've met him as a person, emerging from his own shadow.
Indeed it is remarkable.
Indeed it is to be remarked of my friend Savage that
the desolation of hopes not merely deferred
but by impracticability brutalized
little marred his genial spirit.
How such a one, so circumstanced by parentage—
the mother crippled by disappointment; the father by rotgut and Percodan—
as to blight his prospects, and blacken with untimely frost the buds
of those ambitions justly excited
by manifest powers, graces, and propensities,
should nonetheless display
discrimination not inferior to those we deem wise,
sympathy judicious and above reproach,
is cause for a wonder neither cynicism can besmirch nor incredulity subvert.
In and out of juvy, jacking cars at fifteen,
snorting lines of Adderal, his nostrils stained blue,
kicked out, taken back, kicked out,
busted, paroled, busted again,
straining to reach the shiny object fallen through the grate,
tantalizing, just beyond his fingers,
finding and losing God,
thinking as he rakes the leaves of the linden tree
outside the sublet bungalow
that eating, sleeping, dying are what it's all about,
nothing else, maybe a few sunsets,
forget about sex.

Thought Problem

How strange would it be if you met yourself on the street?
How strange if you liked yourself,
took yourself in your arms, married your own self,
propagated by techniques known only to you,
and then populated the world? Replicas of you are everywhere.
Some are Arabs. Some are Jews. Some live in yurts. It is
an abomination, but better that your
sweet and scrupulously neat self
emerges at many points on the earth to watch the horned moon rise
than all those dolts out there,
turning into pillars of salt wherever we look.
If we have to have people, let them be you,
spritzing your geraniums, driving yourself to the haberdashery,
killing your supper with a blowgun.
Yes, only in the forest do you feel at peace,
up in the branches and down in the terrific gorges,
but you've seen through everything else.
You've fled in terror across the frozen lake,
you've found yourself in the sand, the palace,
the prison, the dockside stews;
and long ago, on this same planet, you came home
to an empty house, poured a Scotch-and-soda,
and sat in a recliner in the unlit rumpus room,
puzzled at what became of you.

Yet Another Scandal

It's all corrupt, of course it is.
The camouflage just confirms the immutable pattern.
The boy from the outskirts,
caressed for his plasticity and powers of abstraction,
is drawn in deeper and deeper, either on Wall Street,
buffered by tall buildings, or in
the sleepy state capitols—
Dover, Tallahassee, Pierre.
Even he is dazzled by miraculous returns on the money.
What he does, though, he does not for money
(which would be sane) but
of course, of course, of course, of course
for love, for the love
his prestidigitations engender
(which is not sane).
Therefore is he choked in the coils
of his being's enormous Ponzi scheme,
and, also, his children turn away
in shock and disrepair.
Which makes me glad
that I let the investigation proceed in a timely fashion.
I opened my offshore accounts to scrutiny.
I turned my wife in.
When the lawyers from Treasury came to my house
to pore over my dictionaries,
I made them coffee and listened to their troubles.

Bright Copper Kettles

Dead friends coming back to life, dead family,
speaking languages living and dead, their minds retentive,
their five senses intact, their footprints like a butterfly's,
mercy shining from their comprehensive faces—
this is one of my favorite things.
I like it so much I sleep all the time.
Moon by day and sun by night find me dispersed
deep in the dreams where they appear.
In fields of goldenrod, in the city of five pyramids,
before the empress with the melting face, under
the towering plane tree, they just show up.
"It's all right," they seem to say. "It always was."
They are diffident and polite.
(Who knew the dead were so polite?)
They don't want to scare me; their heads don't spin like weathervanes.
They don't want to steal my body
and possess the earth and wreak vengeance.
They're dead, you understand, they don't exist. And, besides,
why would they care? They're subatomic, horizontal. Think about it.
One of them shyly offers me a pencil.
The eyes under the eyelids dart faster and faster.
Through the intercom of the house where for so long there was no music,
the right Reverend Al Green is singing,
"I could never see tomorrow.
I was never told about the sorrow."

A School Day in October

I was on the corner of 39th and Park, waiting for a bus,
just standing on the corner, waiting for a bus. A man walked by—
filthy, fragrant, with a mustache like Nietzsche's.
He was screaming about the Dalai Lama.
Then a woman came up to me saying, "Please, mister. Please, mister."
She had a boy in tow
who was wearing a purple hoodie and looked about nine,
still young enough to return a gaze
but not so young that he could count on a complete recovery.
Distressed pieces of paper—
bills of lading, Starburst wrappers, flyers for the Paradise Club—
littered the gutters and swirled in pipsqueak tornados spawned
by taxicabs blasting downtown.
On which of them was it written, I wondered,
that consciousness leaks from the broken seals,
the busted drumcases, the cracks in the housings, the fissures,
and teems viscously across the surfaces of the world?
"Please mister, please mister."
I gave her a dollar. I didn't want to. I was in a mood
to be stupefied by her condition,
but I did feel sad for the kid.
He should have been in school—
it was a school day in October—
and not walking the more punishing blocks of Park Avenue,
the ones below Grand Central Station,
where we came to beg.

Visiting Paris

They were in the scullery talking.
The meadow had to be sold to pay their riotous expenses;
then the woods by the river,
with its tangled banks and snags elbowing out of the water,
had to go; and then the summer house where they talked—
all that was left of an estate once so big
a man riding fast on a fast horse
couldn't cross it in a day. Genevieve. Hortense. Mémé.
The family's last born, whose pale name is inscribed on the rolls
of the Field of the Cloth of Gold. As in the fresco of the Virgin,
where the copper in the pigment oxidizes to trace a thin green cicatrix
along a seam of Her red tunic,
a suspicion of one another furrowed their
consanguine, averted faces.
Why go anywhere at all when it rains like this,
when the trees are sloppy and hooded
and the foot sinks to the ankle in the muddy lane?
I didn't stay for the end of the conversation.
I was wanted in Paris. Paris, astounded by my splendor
and charmed by my excitable manner,
waited to open its arms to me.

Three Persons

That slow person you left behind when, finally,
you mastered the world, and scaled the heights you now command,
where is he while you
walk around the shaved lawn in your plus fours,
organizing with an electric clipboard
your big push to tomorrow?
Oh, I've come across him, yes I have, more than once,
coaxing his battered grocery cart down the freeway meridian.
Others see in you sundry mythic types distinguished
not just in themselves but by the stories
we put them in, with beginnings, ends, surprises:
the baby Oedipus on the hillside with his broken feet
or the dog whose barking saves the grandmother
flailing in the millpond beyond the weir,
dragged down by her woolen skirt.
He doesn't see you as a story, though.
He feels you as his atmosphere. When your sun shines,
he chortles. When your barometric pressure drops
and the thunderheads gather,
he huddles under the overpass and writes me long letters with
the stubby little pencils he steals from the public library.
He asks me to look out for you.

The Descent of Man

My failure to evolve has been causing me a lot of grief lately.
I can't walk on my knuckles through the acres of shattered glass in the streets.
I get lost in the arcades. My feet stink at the soirees.
The hills have been bulldozed from whence cameth my help.
The halfway houses where I met my kind dreaming of flickering lights in the woods
are shuttered I don't know why.
"Try," say the good people who bring me my food,
"to make your secret anguish your secret weapon.
Otherwise, your immortality will be
an exhibit in a vitrine at the local museum, a picture in a book."
But I can't get the hang of it. The heavy instructions fall from my hands.
It takes so long for the human to become a human!
He affrights civilizations with his cry. At his approach,
the mountains retreat. A great wind crashes the garden party.
Manipulate singly neither his consummation nor his despair
but the two together like curettes
and peel back the pitch-black integuments
to discover the penciled-in figure on the painted-over mural of time,
sitting on the sketch of a boulder below
his aching sunrise, his moody, disappointed sunset.

Knowing

Not just because of my cold, cold heart,
pumping absolute zero in the glacial void,
do I not know anyone truly
but also because of them,
because of something unknowable in them.
Maybe it's better this way.
Know one person truly and you know what they know—
what they know about those they truly know
and what the truly known know
about the people they know.
All those lives pouring in through the news feed,
where is it going to end, and how will it end,
wherever it ends?
My wife knows a woman terrified of going blind.
Alone she sits in a room, with all the lights burning—
the 100-watt overhead, the recessed track lighting,
the three gooseneck lamps,
the five halogens she ordered from a catalogue,
the fluorescent work light sporadically sizzling.
The room burns and glows like a convenience store
on an empty highway in the midnight desert.
Groping down the aisles to check her inventory,
waiting for the marauder to enter and rifle the register,
she thinks, This is not a joke.
When this is over, I will tell someone a story about it.

The People I Know

for Rachel Cohen

"Your friendship has meaning for me," the people I know say,
"but you didn't create me. In and of myself,
I'm just like the water pouring through the spillway
or the bird on that wire, bright-yellow, with elegant black piping.
Which is to say, my relationship is not to you
but to my limitless surroundings, and it suffices."
The days when nothing, or nothing much, happens
are the ones they can't forget, the people I know.
They take the car in to get its oil changed,
its tires checked and rotated.
She at the grimy counter and He, out back jimmying
the hydraulic lift, aren't speaking to each other today.
Two people who live in the world, our world,
hate each other everlastingly today.
Anger is blossoming from the heart of the trivial, the pointless.
Self-esteem is leaking and oozing
over the concrete floor to pool around the feet.
Its color is the pink color of anti-freeze. The air is stringent
with the smell of anti-freeze.
"I've experienced that feeling, I've felt that feeling, too,"
the people I know want to say,
but too long have distance, decorum, and self-consciousness governed
the interactions they have with those
who take care of their machines for them to break out
of the cotton-mouthed suffocations of the same,
of their sameness, which is, to be fair, mystifying to them.
"But . . . but . . . it's killing me, Jake, the pain is killing me."
So the people I know wander out

onto Auto Body Avenue, and think about
the explosions of noise on this major artery of their city,
the traffic in the proximate empyrean,
the intricacies of the nitrogen cycle,
the dance of the universe from the atoms to the stars.
The people I know stare into the plate-glass
coffee-shop windows at the abbreviated faces sitting at the counter.
No one can tell me anything more about the people I know
than what I know already about the people I know.
One man I know is dining with a man he knows.
One woman I know has met a woman with her exact name,
who is from Bessarabia,
though she herself is from Ann Arbor, Michigan.
One girl I know is waiting to be born.
One boy I know is taking a nap.

Pacific Fishes of Canada

Commercial salmon fishermen on the central Oregon coast in the late nineteen-seventies and early eighties didn't like the Russians. (No one ever called them the Soviets.) Other Americans didn't like the Russians either. But other Americans didn't like the Russians because the Russians were sinister and totalitarian, and were locked with America in a conflict that was occasioning the Day of Wrath. When it came to Cold War hostility, though, salmon fishermen were skeptical when they weren't ironic, and bitter when they weren't skeptical. Many I knew had been in Vietnam, or had friends or relatives who had been in Vietnam, or both. Others had drifted into fishing from the counterculture of the sixties. Antipathy to highly organized social systems of every kind was widespread among them; making uncomplicated distinctions between Washington and Moscow wasn't. They didn't like the Russians because the Russians parked their ungainly, behemoth, streaked-and-stained rust-bucket factory trawlers on top of the hake schooling offshore in the summer and represented themselves in such a way as to bring ideological discredit to their politics and their civilization.

From the notional, undulating line twelve miles from the shoreline that was the limit of American territory to another line two hundred miles from the shoreline, Pacific fish once available for slaughter by every country in the world belonged exclusively to America now, to take for herself or to dole out under quotas to others. The Magnuson Act of 1976 said so. That their country, along with all the other maritime nations, had engineered, where geography made it possible, the same water grab off their own shores didn't seem to make the Russians any less resentful about being regulated where they had recently fished when and how they wanted. Though the ocean is big, commercial fishing boats still run the danger of interfering with one another because they go where the fish are, and the fish go where the bait is, along the shifting subaqueous borders where the temperature rises or falls with the currents. Accommodating crowding where fish feed among boats running six sixty-foot lines of lures and baited hooks from outrigger poles and trawlers dragging nets and cables the length of five football fields across ten square miles or so of irregularly bottomed ocean required a civility that the Russians were said not to possess. They had a habit while running their gear of cutting off the long tacking against the current of salmon boats engaged in the delicate job of trolling the submerged mountains where king salmon lurked. They also were understood to be piratical. Salmon are significantly less expensive today than they were then because of fish farming. Salmon farming—fertilizing and hatching captured eggs along rivers and bays with the nefarious expectation that the adult fish will swim back to their natal patch of water and let themselves be caught and killed there—was experimental in the seventies. States on the West Coast operated hatcheries to fortify the runs on their rivers, but most of the salmon people ate still came from the wild, and all the salmon people ate were sold as if they came from the wild. They were a prized and protected fish, and a luxury item on menus. That the Russians poached the ones they found in their huge nets instead of throwing them back in the ocean, as the law required them to do, was an article of faith among fishermen. Other sins were also imputed to the Russians: Russian seamanship was lubberly; Russian women worked on Russian crews, and not just as fish cutters; Russian officers drank vodka while working; Russians were on the verge of mutiny. The Coast Guard yeomen who boarded their factory vessels for surprise spot checks had stories they could tell you.

On summer nights, when the stiff wind from the northwest and the choppy, unnerving, exasperating seas that came with it had died down with the setting sun, the salmon fleet curled up on the long pillows of the Pacific swell, waiting for the morning bite. The one- or two-man crews of the little trollers shut down their engines, leaving just their mast lights, and maybe a light on the bow, burning as a precaution to boats that might be navigating the darkness. As beautiful as it was to step out of the cabin and counterbalance against the Pacific on the chill wooden deck and drink in the light offshore wind, with its fugitive odor of fir trees, and listen to the ocean slapping against the hull and hear the creaking and muffled groaning of the sleeping vessel cradled in the long rhythmic risers (corkscrewing slightly and slowly turning the boat around and around), as satisfying as it was to look up at the stars and a crescent moon above the inanimate mist and then look down to see the rising and falling, sharpening and blurring mast lights of the fleet scattered over twenty square miles to the horizon, it was conversely as jarring to see on the same horizon a 300-foot factory ship, an ominous harbinger of industrialized fishing, its 7,000-horsepower diesel engine running nonstop, all its sickly yellow deck lights glaring while its swarming crew processed the tons of hake they had hauled up during the day.

North Pacific hake, also known as Pacific whiting, are a silvery gray fish belonging to the order that includes cod and haddock. Marine mammals eat them. So do mature king salmon, which is why salmon fishermen and Russian fishing vessels fishing in American waters found themselves squaring off. King salmon, also known as Chinook salmon, after the Columbia River Indian tribe who venerate them both before and after they eat them, are the most prized of the anadromous fish species. Anadromous, which comes from the Greek for running upward, means that such fish hatch and smolt in streams and rivers, migrate to the ocean for their half-dozen or so adult years, and then return to spawn and die in the fresh waters where they were born. The struggle to get to those waters was always terrible for the king salmon of the West Coast, and has been more so since modern people built dams on the rivers and polluted the waterways with industrial and agricultural effluvia. Still, some of these salmon suffer the agonies and swim nine hundred miles inland and climb seven thousand feet above sea level to spawn. Salmon fishermen of the mid-to-late seventies and early eighties were a variety of human being whose habits, behaviors, adaptations, and patterns of mind were interesting to me, both to emulate and to observe. They were unique for their general lack of fear of friends, strangers, or themselves. They followed the seasons and identified with the birds and beasts, and knew feast and famine: six months of feast, when the fish were running, and six famine months between November and May, when they scraped by. Sole-proprietor ocean-going agrarians of the by that time largely extinct class which Jefferson would have recognized as his ideal, the real citizens of his imaginary democracy, they were ethnically almost homogenous but at the same time post-tribal and tolerant (because the size, grandeur, and threat of the environment they worked in rendered social distinctions and discriminations trivial, they were the most racially tolerant people I've ever known). Set beside the other populations who made up the Northwest's rural economy—the farmers; the loggers; the ranchers; the mom-and-pop pot growers living in trailers and teepees deep in the Coast Range and the Cascades and practicing a kind of rudimentary countercultural Mormonism at the edge of Forest Service land; the gypo cedar scroungers; the tree planters; the survivalists far up the Yachats or Alsea Rivers, with their canned goods, their smoked deer and elk meat, their subsistence vegetable gardens, and their guns (I remember from that paranoid era a map of the United States that depicted Oregon as the only one of the contiguous forty-eighty states to escape the jet-stream-borne clouds of radioactive fallout resulting from a nuclear war between America and Russia)—salmon fishermen seemed cosmopolitan, practically Parisian.

The Pacific gave them scale, an aesthetic education, and a moral one, also, because on a dangerous medium in a small vessel virtue is important to survival. A dramatic and dramatically visual sense of their lives as enacted in panorama informed their activity and labor. Following the salmon runs, they went down the coast and up: south to Coos Bay, Brookings, Crescent City, Eureka, Fort Bragg, Bodega Bay, and, sometimes, to fish the Sacramento River kings, all the way to the dense shipping lanes pouring the world's cargo through the Golden Gate; or north to Astoria, Ilwaco, and Port Angeles, at the mouth of Puget Sound. Going in and out of a dozen harbors, they came across cocaine smugglers; Mexicans; Filipinos; Chinese; schoolteachers from the Valley who had acquired commercial salmon licenses to moonlight in the summers; prosperous couples from Tiburon, Santa Barbara, or Catalina Island who fitted their fiberglass cruisers with outrigger poles to commercial fish for fun and profit when the weather was balmy and the ocean flat. The shift in perspective that comes from looking at the land from the water made them worldly and detached. The transformation in the motion under their feet, from liquid to solid and back again, altered their minds in expansive ways; so did interchanging, week in and week out, solitude and sociability. Metaphysically alert and double-visioned because they negotiated between two fundamental, antagonistic elements, they were, unusually among people who do risky, physically demanding work, contemplative, introspective, and aware of their own fragility and vulnerability, and that of their species.

· ◆ ·

It had been a while since the years of revolution, but the talk was still all about liberation—not credible negative liberation from, say, privation, tyranny, censorship, and abduction by night, but big American liberation, positive, material and spiritual, paradoxical and unimaginable, crowded around with myths and poems and shot through with a seductive incoherence. Large sections of society were experimenting. Cults multiplied, with some bad consequences. Therapies multiplied. Flying saucers carried people away. Some people were being born again, others were seeing the end of the world. The new music was being made by the Sex Pistols and Devo, and that music was disaffected and conceptual, but in the rural Northwest people were still listening to the old music, which promised freedom. Freedom this and that. Freedom from sexual repression, social norms, war, crude oil, pollution. *I was a free man in Paris. It's knowing that your door is always open and your path is free to walk. So take a good look at my face. Freedom's just another word. There is a town in North Ontario. If you want to know what it is to be free, you have to spend the day in bed with me.*

I'd been hovering around these ideas for as long as I'd known about them. With their glamour and history, they offered camouflage for the endless vacation I was taking from my circumstances and my identity in my late adolescence and early and mid-twenties. Through my partiality to the ideas, I became attached to salmon fishermen. I'd managed to convince myself that only salmon fishermen were liberated from expectations external to themselves. Through my attachment to salmon fishermen, I wound up in late October of 1981 getting more seasick than I'd ever been, so seasick that to this day whenever I'm on or near a commercial dock and smell, however faint it is, that odor characteristic to fishing boats—a perfume synthesized from the fumes of diesel fuel, hydraulic fluid, iodine, and overripe fish—my gorge rises in affliction. I was so seasick then that not long afterward I decided to swear off the ocean forever, except as something to look at and take an occasional dip in.

Fishermen didn't like the Russians, and they were unenthusiastic about other nationalities—Poles, Taiwanese, Koreans, Norwegians—who fished off the Northwest coast. They did, though, admire the Japanese, irrationally (because when it came to practices in American waters that could be interpreted as offensive to American hospitality the Japanese probably weren't any better or worse than anyone else) and almost without qualification. The Japanese were on a roll in those days, in themselves and in the way they were perceived. They had a nice aura. They weren't the defeated nation of the Second World War, and they weren't the inscrutable threat to American economic supremacy that they became in the nineteen-eighties. They were disciplined, intelligent, hardworking pacifists who made excellent, inexpensive products. They were modest and hardy and expert. Knowledge of their profound civilization had penetrated far into the country. People in the fishing industry on the West Coast might not have possessed the details, but they sensed the power of the exquisite imagination. A resource-poor, talent-rich island nation the size of California, with a population of a hundred and twenty or so million, almost half of whose protein came from fish (they ate fish raw and they cooked it; they ate shark meat and, in spite of the indignation, whale meat; they ate fish processed into spongy little cakes called *surimi;* they relished the sexual organs of pollock and perch; they ate blowfish, one of the world's most poisonous vertebrates, which will kill you if you don't handle it just right before you eat it), Japan reacted the only way it could when the establishment of the 200-mile limit began restricting, and in the cases of highly valued fish like salmon and halibut terminating, its access to ground-fish stocks off American shores—it used its strong currency to begin buying up the American fishing industry (a depredation the Russians weren't capable of). This meant that the Japanese were around and available for inspection. Fish-plant owners up and down the coast did business with them. They operated on a large and a small scale, making big deals for all the product of this or that outfit and at the same time stationing themselves on little salmon-buying barges anchored in the bays, where they purchased delicate, roseate, translucent, and mouth-watering pearls of salmon roe directly from the fishing boats and processed them on the spot for shipping to their hungry home world. They ate chowder and chicken-fried steak with fish brokers and local bankers in the bayfront restaurants, and were later commended for their politeness, dainty habits, and clarity of being.

It wasn't, though, their dainty habits that excited the deep, enduring respect felt by people in the fish business for the Japanese; it was their long experience on the Bering Sea. Except for the war years, they'd fished the Bering Sea—which because of the Magnuson Act now belonged to America all the way to the International Date Line—since the nineteen-thirties. Their knowledge of those wild, fabulously rich, frigid waters was unequalled, and their toughness in persisting on them was legendary. They fished the mountainous waves all the way up to the ice line, by day and by night also, when the Northern Lights towered over them. They quailed at nothing. Storm after winter storm battered them. Tremendous Arctic waves cascaded over their tossing vessels. So cold was the air that the moment the water touched the deck, the wheelhouse, and the superstructures it froze. The crews clambered up with baseball bats day and night, high up onto the hook-line booms and gyrating gantries and up the smokestack whipping back and forth in the gale to knock the ice off before the plunging vessel became so top-heavy that it capsized in the next swell.

One evening this past September, I flew along the edge of a lightning storm with a literature professor, who said to me as she looked out the plane's window and saw the black thunderheads running at us and the five-mile-long bolts of lightning cracking earthward in the gloom that there were a lot of aspects of the sublime she could do without. I agree with her now, but in those days some of my illusions had to be pushed to their limits before I could relinquish them. When I heard the stories about the waves like mountains on the Bering Sea and the winter storms when the wind blew ninety knots, I couldn't wait to see it for myself, and see it framed by matter-of-fact Japanese intrepidity—something fatal and irresistible blossomed in my head when I joined the images of the storms with my fantasies of the people. To survey and inventory better waters that were now America's, the National Marine Fisheries Service had since the inception of the Magnuson Act put observers on a small percentage of foreign vessels fishing within the two-hundred-mile limit, to do low-level biological data-gathering of species and distributions. I took a class in ichthyology at Oregon State, in Corvallis, and talked my way into an observer job. After more training in Seattle, I was equipped with a copy of *Pacific Fishes of Canada,* by J. L. Hart, the authority on North Pacific fish, so I could identify such fish; baskets to gather samples of them in such a way as to roughly equal their species distribution overall in a catch; a hanging scale with chains and a hook to weigh them and a tape measure to measure them; scalpels and fish knives, to dissect them and ascertain what sex they belonged to; a blunt knife to crack open their skulls, and tweezers to remove their otoliths—small, hard ovoids of calcium carbonate found in the vestibules of vertebrates, by means of which their age can be determined; little vials and labels to store and classify those otoliths; tiny plastic bags for scale samples; log books to write observations of fishing practices in; log sheets to record latitude, longitude, catch size by metric ton and distribution by species, incidence of species forbidden to foreign vessels (salmon, halibut, king crab, tanner crab, opilio crab, Dungeness crab), sightings of marine mammals, etc.; and a heavy blue short-wave radio transmitter that transmitted not voices but numbers only, into which I was told to input every week the metric tonnages of targeted species caught, so that the Fisheries Service could extrapolate and thereby monitor their quotas.

A plane flew me north to Anchorage, and a van drove me to Seward, at the head of Resurrection Bay, a spectacular fjord on the scrubby, desolate Kenai Peninsula, which had huge fish hawks plummeting for salmon into its waters. There, the *Akebono Maru No. 11,* a small stern trawler with a crew of thirty-three belonging to a small Tokyo trading company called Nichiro Gyogyo-Kabushiki Kaisha Ltd., steamed in to fetch me just ahead of the first of the Gulf of Alaska winter storms. While I was being taken out to the boat in a Zodiac, over water that was already choppy and windswept,

I could see the leading edge of the front rolling up the fjord. I'd expected and, because I'd been land bound for four months and knew my sea legs were gone, had wanted the boat to anchor until the storm blew over, but after welcoming me and receiving my credentials when I came on board the captain, a shrewd, rotund man from Yokohama with an inexpressibly soft handshake, turned the vessel around into the teeth of the southerly. I got sick before I could stow my gear in the tiny cabin I was assigned, sick in a way I'd never been sick before, seasick without respite, for days. Imagine the body not only convulsively throwing up the contents of its stomach in a spasm of all its muscles but heaving to expel the stomach itself through the esophagus (every sixty seconds or so at first), while the brain turns to mush with dizziness and vertigo. At running speed in heavy twenty-foot seas, the impact of the bow of a 140-foot boat on a rising swell is tremendous. Lying down had always been a weak, temporary, but slightly effective respite from seasickness for me. Every time, though, that I tried to wedge myself into my bunk, which was built for someone three-quarters my size, the boat would lurch, and I'd be thrown out on the floor, to lie there rolling and groaning in my own vomit. The assault on my vestibular system was so bad that even my sinuses were dizzy. I felt that I was going to throw up through my nose.

The cabin boy came in to help me clean up. I was shivering, sweating, dehydrating rapidly, retching continuously, and hideously unbalanced. All I could tolerate was water, and that only because I understood, even in my misery, that it was dangerous to vomit convulsively when the stomach was empty. The cabin boy insisted I consume grapefruit, and left me Mandarin oranges, apples and persimmons wrapped in their own netting, small cans of citric-flavored liquid vitamins, packages of the Japanese equivalent of Melba toast. I threw up the grapefruit and stuck to the water, which I also threw up the moment it hit my stomach.

I couldn't keep myself in the bunk and spent the first day on the floor. The wind picked up to sixty knots, so the boat throttled down and wallowed in heavy seas, which made the nausea more intense and unbearable. The officers came in to offer me sympathy. For the three days the storm and my sickness lasted they entered my cabin and annoyed me with their solicitude. The captain came in and implored me by means of little coughs and gestures to consume more than water. The first officer brought me English toffee from his private hoard, along with more grapefruit. The radio officer came in and gave me a small bottle of sake and a conspiratorial grin.

At six in the morning, twelve noon, six in the evening, and midnight, the cabin boy knocked politely on my door and informed me that the officers had invited me to share a meal in their cramped mess. On the morning of the fourth day, when I felt less ectoplasmic, when I felt I had gathered enough substance, and when the storm had died and the boat was fishing again, far down the Aleutians, I finally made it to the mess and was greeted with hilarity. The seamen on watch came in to introduce themselves. Polite as they were, they couldn't help but find my condition funny. The cabin boy showed me off like his newborn baby, and then gave me rice and a piece of dried fish. The first officer joined me in the cramped booth and was served a bowl of long, fluted, cream-colored yarns of flesh bathed in what looked like ponzu sauce. When I was given to understand, by means of the few English and Japanese words we had in common and many gestures involving comparative anatomy, that these were that rare delicacy the gonads of male pollock—pollock were the main target species of the boat—I barely made it to the head in time to throw up.

· ◆ ·

Below decks, forward the bulkhead that separated the waist from the forecastle of the *Akebono Maru No. 11*, there was a makeshift version of a traditional Japanese bath (about the size of a small walk-in closet with a low ceiling) reserved for the officers, to which class I temporarily belonged. A tap with a rubber hose that ended in a shower head rose from a freshwater tank below the ferrocement floor, which was covered with slatted, movable wooden rectangles, approximately two-by-two feet. Squeezed in next to the tap stood a long, deep copper tub filled with sea water heated to the extremity of human tolerance. At five-thirty every afternoon, I padded down in the straw sandals and terrycloth kimono provided by the boat, washed myself thoroughly and quickly in precious fresh water, inched into the hot-salt-water tub, and steeped myself in the recurring thought that I was one of Melville's isolatoes, a race unto myself, a country unto myself, a far-flung island nation in a frigid ocean, battered by storms and mountainous waves, towered over by the shimmering Northern Lights. Spinning literary conceits like this one was a habitual occupation of mine on the boat. In the oceanic tedium, I would bounce them against my mind like a kid playing catch with a wall. I had a lot of time on my hands. My duties were made light by the regular interference of weather bad enough to limit fishing; and even when the weather was good my duties were light enough to give me plenty of time to indulge my invented self, my sea-going fictional self, and wallow in my version of the well-documented affliction that causes people to live in literature rather than life.

On clement days, the boat, when it wasn't in transit, ran four shifts of six hours each, half the crew on and half off, and hauled the gear on average twice a shift. I was in my cabin reading Shackleton's account of his Antarctic expedition or *Gravity's Rainbow* or *Hopscotch*, or in my cabin just waking up, or on the bow watching the frigate birds, petrels, and goofy albatrosses, or playing Go in the mess with one of the junior officers, or in the radio room listening for hours to Voice of America on the shortwave. The situation in Poland was getting worse and worse. Solidarity, feeling the people and the church behind it, demanded revolution. Moscow, hidden in the shadows, instructed its clients in the government. General Jaruzelski imposed martial law. The Polish Army took to the streets, the factories, the coal mines. On the Long Range Navigation charts used by all vessels then to determine their position on the sea, there were channels clearly marked as submarine transit lanes, where boats were forbidden to drop their gear. Up the coast and down, up through the Bering Sea and under the ice of the Chukchi Sea, submarines with nuclear-tipped missiles were sensing one another with their sonar, circling one another, playing war games. A bell went off, the winches began working to spool in their warps, and I put on my rain gear. When the big steel otter boards that held the net mouth open in the water clanged onto the deck, I clambered out through a hatch in the stern and watched the bulging, dripping purse of fish being hauled in over the stern ramp and lifted up by hook lines and emptied on the deck.

When the weather was flat, the crew would horse around on the deck. If a particularly interesting creature turned up in the catch—a six-foot long halibut, say, or a giant squid, or a bevy of lumpsuckers, which when their swim bladders distend in the air are the size and shape of softballs (with little fins) and look alarmingly like the heads of newborn human infants—they would make me lie down on the deck next to the monsters and then click away with their Minoltas as if the monsters and I were Notre Dame and they were on their European vacations. If, though, the weather was rough—and they fished in very rough weather—they were almost inconceivably efficient and graceful in their work. The net came over the ramp, bulging and dripping, the hook lines were attached, the winch on the boom lifted the bag over the deck, the rope that released the valve of the cod end was yanked, the catch tumbled out. The valve was hammered back in and the net went back down the ramp. The warp spooled out again, the otter boards were dropped, and the boat recommenced fishing. All this was done with speed and economy.

Before the fish were funneled into the broad hatch over the fish bin in the stern, I separated out the forbidden species, measured them, took scale samples from the salmon if there were any, and returned them to the sea. I went down the little hatch and collected my baskets, which I had positioned randomly in the fish bin and which had been retrieved by a crew member before they were buried in fish. I filled two more baskets separately with the target species, to size and sex them. While the crew began dressing fish in the small workspace in the stern and packaging them for the blast freezers below, I went to my work station and amassed and recorded my data. If the target species in the area we were in was pollock, my sample baskets were clean and uninteresting. Pollock swim mostly by themselves, except for the halibut and salmon that feed on them, in the middle range of the water column. If the target species was Atka mackerel or yellowfin sole, which the boat fished from the sea floor with a drag net, the sample baskets were filled with odd, fascinating specimens: sand-lances; prowfish; quillfish; thorny, great, sailfin, grunt, and ribbed sculpins; various members of the tasty Scorpaenidae family—darkblotched rockfish, dusky, silvery-gray, rougheye, and redbanded rockfish, blues, tigers, ocean perch; the eelpout, the clingfish, the viperfish; dolly vardens (named after a character in *Barnaby Rudge*); spine eels, gunnels, pricklebacks; starry skates and black skates; dogfish; greenlings; lingcod; rattails; capelins; flathead sole and arrowtooth flounder.

· ◆ ·

There were two kinds of idleness on the *Akebono Maru*. The first was pleasant and expansive. The boat was running in fresh weather from one fishing ground to another, or, with the ocean flat, had retired to the leeward side of one of the Aleutians to rendezvous with a transport vessel and spend a day offloading fish and taking on supplies under the protection of an extinct volcano. Though we were far north and in the darkest months of the year, those days left an impression of balminess. They were relaxed and social and the crew was happy. The other idle times occurred when the weather stormed. These times became more frequent as January approached. The sky boiled over with darkness, the waves topped out at forty feet, the wind gusted to ninety knots. We were in the birthplace of the West Coast winter storms, and when they blew they blew day after day after day. All the boat could do was nose into the swell to keep from being broadsided by the waves. Officers and crew became tense, fearful, and morose. Their faces were stripped of conviviality, and then of their stoicism, and on them could now be discerned misgivings about their fate, a consciousness of the bitterness of their lives—nine months a year spent on the high seas, doing harsh, dangerous, physical work six hours on, six hours off, day in and day out, enduring the planet's worst weather, enduring endless blowing and buffeting. For what? At meals, the first officer would pour a generous shot of Suntory whiskey in a tall glass, which he then filled with Kirin beer and drained down, and then would do the same thing a few times more before staggering off down the pitching passageways to his bunk.

When the weather was good, I moved through the day feeling my destiny fulfilled, feeling transcendent. Just by being where I was, I had arrived at the pinnacle of my life on earth. The globe we live on, its lands and creatures, rolled below me as an extension of myself. I'd found my balance on the rolling floor, and it was as if I had my balance for the first time, and as if that balance were absolute, were itself a kind of perception comprising all the senses, and unifying them at this pinpoint of being. I'd accomplished what I was meant to accomplish—though I didn't know what this exactly was—and had arrived at a mysterious and cosmic inner intersection, the outward embodiment of which was the great intersection of sea and sky. Just by being where I was, I'd made myself new. When the weather was bad, though—and the weather was mostly bad—I had the opposite experience. The word misgivings couldn't begin to comprehend the mortification I felt at being on a boat on the Bering Sea in this kind of weather. The crew might have been morose, but they knew where they came from and where they belonged. I, obviously, knew neither. I was pathetic, living someone else's life because I didn't have one of my own. In the gloom at the edge of the world, my recklessness became apparent to me, my foolish pursuit of extremes, my childish confusions of life and literature, my fabrications and fantasies—Jeffersonian democracy and salmon fishing, the Bering Sea, the Japanese! What would become of my poor immigrant parents if I drowned out here?

One twilight off the Pribilof Islands, when the wind was rising and the boat had pulled the gear and was waiting on a storm, I went up to the bridge and stared out at an ocean growing wilder and wilder. A thousand yards away, a small fishing boat, a longliner—the first boat we had encountered in the past months, except for the transports and a Coast Guard vessel that had tried and failed to board us in rough weather in Unimak Pass—was toiling south in the gloom and the heavy waves, yawing up to its gunnels and inching forward, gasping in the growing swell. For some reason, nothing has ever given me a more powerful sense of human pathos and desolation, nothing has given me a deeper education in despair, than seeing that longliner working in that emptiness. I still shudder when I remember it. I hurried back down to my cabin and didn't leave for a day. When I couldn't stand lying in my bunk anymore, I reluctantly emerged. We were by that time in a full gale. I went back up to the bridge and stared out at the Pribilofs, which appeared, miles off, at the top of each swell we were nosing into and disappeared as we plunged into the trough. I said to myself, "I'm an Indian. What am I doing here?" I said it over and over. It wasn't exactly what I meant to say to myself. Despair tends to cloud insight, and makes thought imprecise. But, in fact, what I meant to say exactly I have yet to find words for.

Personal Essay

I'm not sure where to start, so I'll start by italicizing the *difference*
between the experience I find compelling enough
to imagine sitting at a screen writing about it
and the experience that is its polar opposite
(which is compelling, too,
though in a way that leaves me disinclined to express myself in words,
that tends to annihilate words),
the experience by which we become aware that what we see, smell, hear, feel, taste,
substance in its impressions,
what our machines record,
what we theorize and what our theories predict,
our books and monographs remember,
substance in its forms,
our brains dream as they flicker in the dark—
the magnolias and protons, the cephalopods and nucleotides,
the sweet ripe peach, dripping honey,
the salmon trollers anchored up in the cove,
circumnavigating themselves with the ebbing tide,
the sockeye salmon running Bristol Bay,
the Gulf Stream, the Van Allen radiation belt,
the historical figures
(Ted Williams, Begum Akhtar, Shaka Zulu, Don Ho,
Carl Phillip Emmanuel Bach bowing to the Hohenzollern
Prince-Elector later known as Fredrick the Great),
the black basalt temple,
the solitary black temple that sits on the blinding white shore,
or creatures such as the Gorgon in its lair,
the Son of the Morning Star,
the Celestial Dragon, Mara Lord of Death—
don't *resemble* anything. They're just themselves, they're only themselves.

They might multiply across the universe, but they don't *correspond*
to anything, neither do they
symbolize anything, *allegorize* anything,
they *embody* nothing but themselves,
and so they are what we call abstractions,
which makes us abstractions in an abstract world—
though that sounds too much like the discredited
twentieth century talking,
and though the words *abstract* and *abstraction* imply the *concretion*
the reality of which the insight that lies embedded in this experience,
and is both its cause and effect,
is the serpent that eats its own tail,
exactly obliterates. I turn down my street tonight.
The streetlight behind me throws my shadow in front of me.
I'm suddenly—what's the word?—*bemused.*
I'm bemused because I think I'm not what I think I am—
whatever I think I am—
but am in fact an object, a thing,
one more thing that throws a shadow, and has
extension, dimension, limitation. And also the thing that I am
is not a shadow of something else, or a shadow of a shadow
of something else, that's not the way it works,
but is itself only.
To see the self as it is, a phenomenon in space,
perpendicular to the rays of a streetlight sweeping the corner,
a torch in a cave, a searchlight at a border crossing,
a beacon, a flashlight, the sun . . .
You understand what I mean, you others,
or understand at least how shocking the obvious can be
if you're not ready for it.

A thing, an artifact wrapped in its artifactuality,
an anthology of arbitrary gestures made by space—
which itself is active not passive, itself something and not nothing—
a congeries of angles and broken lines,
maybe not nothing but
not the image of anything but the image of
nothing, a face astonished by itself in the mirror
(that couldn't be me, could it?),
a body on a gurney that sits up
and makes claims that scare the attending medical personnel.
Why didn't somebody tell me about this?
Simultaneously, the universe cracks,
and through the crack the mind
returns in vapors to the chrysalis of nonexistence
from which it once crawled, blinking,
to find that what they told it was real
was, in fact, real:
the mossy, leaf-strewn lane canopied by beech trees was real,
and the hedgerow with the little five-barred gate.
The scent of honeysuckle floated from the garden on the other side,
from which garden was heard voices and the sound of birds.
But the mind couldn't enter—
the mind was too big or, maybe, it was too small.
Something about the dimensions wasn't right.
Something wasn't scalable.
The garden, the garden, with voices, and the sound of birds.
What's a child, a mere child, to do in a world
ravaged by war and plague?
God of visions, speak to me, and say why I should worship thee.
And on Atlantic Avenue, in a cab going to the airport,

almost the same thing happens again, and again.
If you don't travel much by air, as I don't,
if your job has been, as mine has been, to hollow out of rock,
with a tenacity that surprises even you,
a little indentation, a dimple
(scraping and scraping with your inadequate devices)
a place to put your suction cups down, get a grip,
so you can spread at your other end
the filaments of your being, which will transmit
the waves of energy swelling around you, billowing and subsiding—
storms of radiance, solar flares, fountains, typhoons,
blizzards of the infinitesimal particles shooting to China
(on the other side of the planet!),
so empty, latticed, and fashioned out of negative space is earth to them,
which seems so dense to us—
the thought of going to JFK and climbing into a narrow metal tube
that by an artifice that could be called infernal
will lift itself to thirty thousand feet
and speed at six hundred miles an hour through the troposphere
can, if not handled tactfully within yourself,
lead to anxious feelings.
Slowly, painfully, consciousness decouples from the room it has lain in
with a cold compress over its eyes.
Slowly, reluctantly, it goes down the interior staircase, then the stoop to the street
with the tidy single-family dwellings and neighbors who are hard-working.
Carefully and curiously does it observe these neighbors,
couples and single people
loitering outside on this warm but not humid day.
Clumsily it struggles to recollect their histories,
and vaguely it remembers, or does it?

He was the son of the family who owned the mill
and the big house on the hill.
She was the milkmaid shy as a fawn.
They met in the pasture as the fireflies came on.
A teardrop fell from her eye.
When they touched, they heard the earth sigh.
An emerald glory consumed them both,
and they ran away together in the teeth of . . . I forget what . . . ,
mute, ecstatic, terrified,
only to wind up here,
on a street with Sam, who is sitting on his porch in an unfolded folding chair,
and Frank and Louise, and the old lady
from Palermo whose name I can never remember—
fifty years she's lived in Brooklyn and still
doesn't know more than a dozen words of English—
and Stan and Ann,
waving at me from their window bye-bye, bye-bye.
Who are these people, really,
and how could I have taken them for granted?
What do they know, and when do they know it?
Were they planted here? This much is obvious: they're not
who they say they are.
Their identities are either accidents or conspiracies, which are the same.
What, though, are their essences?
Slowly consciousness estranges itself from those with whom
proximity, if not propinquity, has caused it to
identify, and slowly the consciousness estranges itself
from everything else that identifies it—
the place it lives, or at least tries to live.
The things—the cars, the trees, the brick house fronts, the garbage cans—

are glowing not by natural light, reflected from the sun,
which seems a little distracted today,
but out of their own beings,
not from without but from within—
red brick, sheet metal pounded thin, galvanized tin.
Clouds oversized, exaggerated in the pale sky, drawn with a crayon by a kid,
which confirms that we are in a fabrication, maybe even in a mistake,
maybe even in a cartoon.
Slowly the mind finds itself in a cab,
slowly the mind finds itself in a cab on Atlantic Avenue,
suddenly it occurs to the mind that the fact they make people live here,
on Atlantic Avenue, reveals as nothing else can
the criminality of the social order.
Along the wound that is Atlantic Avenue from Flatbush to the sea—
hacked out by a blunt axe, disfiguring the earth—
they pack them in by the tens of thousands
and surround them with discount tire outlets and disreputable used-car dealers . . .
broken, unfathomable streets
spreading out into Bed-Stuy and Crown Heights . . .
gloom under the elevated tracks of the Long Island Railroad,
with which tracks a malevolent municipal authority
has chosen to stitch this thoroughfare
for miles and miles . . .
dismay in the undergirders spattered by mourning doves,
lamenting in the crevices . . .
who here doesn't understand what they mean when they talk about
the tears of things? . . .
despair collapsing on itself . . . unbearable . . .
lives that could be our lives . . . maybe they are our lives . . .
An old man walks into a storefront dialysis clinic.

He's the only person on the street,
and it's not exactly dawn and carillon bells ringing "Ave Maria" around here.
The sidewalks are menacing. The crummy bodegas are gated and locked.
The windows of the sagging tenements are thick with dust.
Poor old guy, too sick to work.
Does he live alone, or with family?
Does he get Social Security? Medicare? Dialysis isn't cheap.
Who pays to have his blood washed and dried
three times a week? Who takes him out to the ballgame?
As long as I've known myself, I've been here, right here, old man,
sitting in a cab at the corner of Atlantic and Troy
on my way to JFK,
looking at you and asking these melancholy questions,
and never have I got an answer that is anything more than
an affront to my rationality,
and I'm not going to get one today, no, or even get the
emollient effect sympathy for suffering creation
has on the leather of the soul, making it soft and pliable,
or the thrill of righteousness
that comes from imagining myself wasting the tyrant authors of your condition—
the minions of darkness who isolate us from one another.
But, instead, the moment is becoming
dangerous and cosmic.
One train of thought has left the sidings, but the next
hasn't been shunted on, and here is the gap where we are, the interregnum
where we are, one more time, the edge
of the forgotten village. West Virginia or Kansas
knows no desolations more weedy and forlorn than this,
the empty train yard of your mind,
its adjacencies overgrown with nettles and goldenrod,

dusty ailanthus, a sunflower
beside the mounded gravel of the trackside banks,
shimmering white in steady sunshine. It is hot.
The one-armed switchman has gone home to lunch.
He lives in the village. They practice the old-time religion there.
They sip lemon squash in the summertime.
And the mind must inflate to fill the empty yard
that is the mind,
and as it balloons what it has been looking at
in detachment, indifference, curiosity, compassion, excitement,
rage, inertia, boredom, awe
shrinks inversely, deflates and collapses—
it is not what it is; it never was what it was.
And then, one more time, on cue,
the strange elongations begin, the self's hundred lines converge,
that which is not finite, that which is as it is,
that which they have called (how long have they called it that?)
absolute, uninflected,
without privation of any sort or kind,
the hundred names, none of which we speak because they burn our lips,
stumbles in to laminate to permanence
the now forever uncanny street, the old man, the bodega, the
nephrology clinic . . .
self-sustaining in its self love . . . please, call it whatever you want . . .
to which we are told to "Bow down, young man, bow down" . . .
terminally boring, drunk on its own tedium, its absences,
its absence of dimension, of borders, of limitations,
its enormity and its Oneness,
which it is so, so proud of, embodied in waterfalls of nothingness
inundating the small and self-contained,

the objects huddled in their privacies,
crushing them, making them unrecognizable,
stamping out of them all the sweet and reasonable similitudes,
all the pathetic, clinging analogies.
Stare at a word in a book long enough and that word
slowly uncouples itself from what it means.
The meaning backs away.
The meaning is being evicted from
the structure of glyphs that it has rented.
The meaning of the word is making
dejected, wounded gestures with its hands as it retreats
to the precipice of the incomprehensible, where it gives us
a tender look, then turns and jumps.
Its survivors are dangling lines, circles, serifs, italic or roman, standard or bold.
Look at an old man on a street with fixed concentration and he resolves
into his colors and shapes and durations.
He's arbitrary. He's accidental.
He could have been put together in a number of ways.
Why this instead of that? He could be a toy. He is a toy, but whose?
Look at his neighborhood with the concentration of an eight-year-old
and slowly it resolves to a composition comprising
rectangles, triangles, boxes, lines, polygons, convex polygons,
parallelograms, rhomboids, quadrilaterals, pyramids,
dodecagons, hexagons, octagons,
stars of Lakshmi, arbelos,
deltoids, Archimedean spirals,
magatamas, triquetras, Yin-Yangs.
Squash them together any way you want.
You can follow the instructions and make them into shapes
with sharp angles, or collapse them into mounds—

termite mounds, mud huts,
abandoned mud dwellings camouflaged to resemble the ochre rock
to which they cling,
high up on the cliff where the condor once nested
and the desert wind moaned through the apertures.
These edifices are actually as tiny as they look,
as tiny as you are huge.
Their size depends on your size. The fact that they are is what either
gladdens or terrifies,
depending on your mood, and is what
can't be controlled or understood.
Later, on the plane, it gets even worse.
To have become so big that they can see it all at a distance
and even turn the wrong end of the telescope on themselves
suggests a recklessness, not to speak of a stupidity,
for which humans should be punished to the end of time.
Toy cars with the toy people inside them going to the doll houses
that are resolving themselves into their mere geometries.
The toy train tracks and the toy skyscrapers.
Yes, it's true, the world is ugly and the people are sad,
but that's OK, isn't it?
Then, looking down at the cars and houses from five thousand feet,
maybe it is not—lumps of substance
flattening now to indentations in the pool of radiation,
dimples in the whorls of energy
sucked through the stars,
splatters from the torn fabric that cradled the spreading plasma,
mercuric, molten, silver arterial fire.
It doesn't have a purpose, whoever said it did?
It disappoints me, I have to admit it.

I should feel joy, awe, I should feel overwhelmed by
the mystery, but I'm sorry, I don't.
I like the palm trees and the Day-Glo colors of Las Vegas.
When I went there as a youngster, I wasn't disappointed.
Hawaii didn't disappoint me either.
When I saw it a few years ago,
improbable as it was, Hawaii was so much more fantastic than
anything I'd imagined for the decades I'd imagined it.
But when I look down at this and see
how exactly the productions of time appear to timelessness
(eternity is in love with time),
the dispensations of space to infinity,
when I see everything reduced to abstractions,
see that nothing represents or imitates, finds safety by looking
like something else, but instead stands out
in its rancorous individuation,
when I realize it's not just the story I want that I'm not going to get
but that I am not going to get any story at all,
only its false climaxes, unable to resolve—
I am disappointed, d-i-s-a-p-p-o-i-n-t-e-d, disappointed
at what I'm willing to call, because of I'm tired of trying to think it through,
the purposelessness, the pointlessness,
the suffocating blankness, the emptiness that is not and is not
and is not empty but full of emptiness,
and am disappointed, also, that I can't use language to understand
and conclude, finally, but only
to name, itemize, enumerate, classify.
The plane banks north.
It will overfly the Gold Coast, Block Island, Nantucket, Wellfleet,
Boston, Halifax, Gander.

We're going over the Pole, to the Old World.
When we get there, it will be morning here. But to circle back
to the beginning, to what I said was
the experience that I sat down to write about,
the polar opposite of the experience
you've been hearing about, which is actually not one experience but many.
The experience that is the point of this exercise—
the true subject of this . . . what to call it? . . . this *piece of writing*—
is not many experiences masquerading as one
but one experience masquerading as one.
Here it is:
Sometimes at night, in bed, after a more than
usually intricate day of frustrations and sporadic satisfactions,
when I can't fully unplug,
and am feeling put upon, unravelled,
grieving slightly without knowing why, without having a reason,
when I'm not completely dialed down,
when the current is unstable through my wiring
and the amperage surges in fits,
when the needles jump erratically, sometimes into the red zone itself,
I lie back on my pillow and try to smooth it all out.
My eyes are closed.
My clothes are carelessly draped on the chair next to the bed.
While my body is draining down in clockwise spirals to
the spillway, the sluices, the millrace,
to the river, the estuary, the gulf, and into the ocean,
my mind hovers in its trance,
paralyzed whether to stay or go.
The indecision is delicious. Meanwhile, a thought is forming.
But this thought, this thought, is not any thought,

not one of the ordinary thoughts,
and definitely not one of the afflicting, defeating, deadly thoughts.
This thought is the one thought, the one insight
that all my life, people, wherever I've lived, whatever I've done,
whoever I've been, I have been waiting for.
Believe me when I tell you it will transform me and save the world.
Look at it, look how large it is, and fine,
composed, graphic, tense with energy, simple yet elegant, and so obvious.
What took me so long to think it?
Before, though, I can grab its tail, its head scuttles
into nonbeing. Before I can remember it,
I have to remember to remember it,
and remember to remember to remember.
The struggle to recollect that there is something to recollect replaces always
the struggle to recollect, which itself has replaced the recollection.
I wasn't fast enough. I'm never fast enough,
and the dissipating phosphorescent track of logic that is
the wake of the thought of which there is not even a memory leaves
a faint, evanescing beauty lingering on the spreading waters.
So, again, this is the scene:
I am lying on my back in bed. My body is paralyzed.
On the great ball rolling back and forth between waking and sleeping,
I am balancing,
backpedaling when it rolls forward, running in place when it rolls back.
This is the moment, if I'm lucky, if I can
keep my balance, neither wake up or fall asleep, that the waters part
and I see the faces.
Or, actually, one face, one face to start.
The face is one I don't know, usually, but sometimes I know it—
my former student Jeannine's, say,

or Herbert Lom's as Napoleon
in the King Vidor movie of *War and Peace,*
with Mel Ferrer, Audrey Hepburn, and Henry Fonda,
as, respectively, Andre, Natasha, and Pierre.
How much have others suffered so that Herbert Lom can learn
what he always knew?
How much so that Mel, Audrey, and Hank can?
How many people have had to die at Marengo and Austerlitz, in the snow,
in the retreat across the Berezina
for them to find themselves in celluloid?
"I who put to death the ancient republic of Venice,"
Herbert is saying. He looks both proud and bitter.
But his face never remains his face,
Jeannine's never remains hers,
or the unknown face the unknown face.
They don't, though, resolve into their constituent geometric parts,
they don't abstract.
Instead, they transmute into other faces unknown to me—
a Berber tribesman,
a pharmacist in Duluth at the turn of the last century,
a woman of the Sudan, or Siberia, or the Yakima valley—
and the transmutations multiply,
faces multiplying by the thousands overlaid on the initiating face,
each vivid, each arresting,
each taking up exactly the time it should before it becomes another face,
Polynesian faces or Swedish faces,
Canary Island, Swiss, Ugandan, or Chinese.
But their identity is not the point,
this is not a nocturnal Family of Man, it's-a-small-world-after-all video,
and neither am I expressing here, with this peroration,

my love for humankind.
It's not a small world after all, that's not the point.
The world is huge and unbearable to think about, and maybe it should be,
maybe it should be the endlessly receding horizon that it is,
which we run after. Who knows?
But, also, from where I'm writing this just a small, manageable interval
of leisurely, meditative travel in an automobile
will bring you to a cliff side overlooking the eastern ocean.
The fog and mist always blow there in the early morning,
and when the sun rises it rises
behind a billowing, shimmering, diaphanous, upward-falling
veil of water particles that
filters the electromagnetic storm of the sun, so that the sun appears
not blinding and burning to the eyes, but as
a pure white disk the exact size of the moon,
into which you can stare and stare.
To look straight into the sun risen behind the mist
is the point of the exercise,
and it is the experience, also, endless and absorbing, of the faces.
They're bright, vivid, alert, and are their own anthems.
They're wrapped and wrapped tight around themselves
as the quarter-mile of yarn that makes a baseball
is wrapped and wrapped around its cork-and-rubber core,
as the plasmic sun is wrapped around
its even more plasmic core, exploding in thermonuclear joy.
That is how it is looking at these faces.
They might be expressing pain in the way they look, suffering even,
or for that matter pleasure, ecstasy, cunning, bliss. But these aren't
things that make us afraid, they're just
elaboration of their vitality, which has pressure, power, immediacy,

and glows. Old and young alike, as they say.
And days afterward, after I have felt the curious release from being human
that these faces give me, and have been
drowned in them and resurrected and drowned again
on the verge of some other sleep, I will be sitting at a meeting,
or on the subway,
or in the Greek coffee shop around the corner where I sometimes eat breakfast,
and someone will give me a look, and I will look back
at his or her face and think, Didn't I see that in a trance?
And I did, I did, I did see it in a trance.

Light Verse

(Standard Time begins)

It's just five, but it's light like six.
It's lighter than we think.
Mind and day are out of sync.
The dog is restless.
The dog's owner is sleeping and dreaming of Elvis.
The treetops should be dark purple,
but they're pink.

Here and now. Here and now.
The sun shakes off an hour.
The sun assumes its pre-calendrical power.
(It is, though, only what we make it seem.)
Now in the dog-owner's dream,
the dog replaces Elvis and grows bigger
than that big tower

in Singapore, and keeps on growing until
he arrives at a size
with which only the planets can empathize.
He sprints down the ecliptic's plane,
chased by his owner Jane
(that's not really her name), who yells at him
to come back and synchronize.

Acknowledgments

Grateful acknowledgment is made to the following publications and sites, in which many of these poems first appeared: *Epiphany* ("Elegy," "The Dream I Didn't Have"); *Fence* ("Secret Police"); *Field* ("Mixed-Media Botanical Drawing," "Trailing Clouds of Glory"); *The New Yorker* ("Memoir," "Family Happiness," "This Morning," "Thought Problem," "Visiting Paris," "Rereading"); *The New York Times* ("Light Verse"); *Ploughshares* ("Guide for the Perplexed"); Plume.org and *The Plume Anthology* ("Nursing Home," "New Media," parts 2 and 3 of "Three Urdu Poems"); *Poetry* (part 1 of "Three Urdu Poems," "Bright Copper Kettles," "Life of Savage," "Three Persons," "Imaginary Number," "Hell," "Purgatory, the Film," "Purgatory, the Sequel," "Heaven"); Poets.org—the web site of the Academy of American Poets ("The Descent of Man"); *A Public Space* ("Knowing"); *The Unexpected Guest*—the publication of the 2012 Liverpool, England, Biennial of Art ("Surveillance Report").

The author would also like to thank the Lower Manhattan Cultural Council, the John Simon Guggenheim Memorial Foundation, and the MacDowell Colony for the Arts for their generosity in providing space, financial resources, and time essential to the completion of this book.

Vijay Seshadri was born in Bangalore, India, and came to America as a small child. He is the author of three other collections of poems, *Wild Kingdom; The Long Meadow,* winner of the James Laughlin Award of the Academy of American Poets; and *The Disappearances* (HarperCollins India), and many essays, reviews, and memoir fragments. He is currently the Myers Professor of Writing at Sarah Lawrence College and lives in Brooklyn, New York.

Book design by Ann Sudmeier. The text typeface is Warnock Pro, a font designed by Robert Slimbach and named after John Warnock, the co-founder of Adobe Systems. Composition by BookMobile Design and Digital Publisher Services, Minneapolis, Minnesota. Manufactured by Versa Press on acid-free 30 percent post-consumer wastepaper.